MW01282376

Bow Hunting for Kids

By

Isiah Maxwell

© Copyright 2018

All rights reserved.

The content contained within this book may not be reproduced, duplicated or transmitted without direct written permission from the author or the publisher.

Under no circumstances will any blame or legal responsibility be held against the publisher, or author, for any damages, reparation, or monetary loss due to the information contained within this book. Either directly or indirectly.

Legal Notice:

This book is copyright protected. This book is only for personal use. You cannot amend, distribute, sell, use, quote or paraphrase any part, or the content within this book, without the consent of the author or publisher.

Disclaimer Notice:

Please note the information contained within this document is for educational and entertainment purposes only. All effort has been executed to present accurate, up to date, and reliable, complete information. No warranties of any kind are declared or implied. Readers acknowledge that the author is not engaging in the rendering of legal, financial, medical or professional advice. The content within this book has been derived from various sources. Please consult a licensed professional before attempting any techniques outlined in this book.

By reading this document, the reader agrees that under no circumstances is the author responsible for any losses, direct or indirect, which are incurred as a result of the use of information contained within this document, including, but not limited to, — errors, omissions, or inaccuracies.

Table Of Contents

Introduction

I want to thank you for choosing this book – '*Bow Hunting for Kids*'

A modern hunter has an arsenal of weapons that he can use to attack his prey. Of all the weapons that a hunter can use, the most challenging and interesting weapon is the bow. Our ancestors used bow hunting as a way to hunt their prey. This goes to show that bow hunting has a huge history. The tools used by modern hunters are certainly more advanced and different from the tools used in the Stone Age. The skills needed to succeed at bow hunting remain the same.

Arrows penetrate deeper and fly further today than they did a thousand years ago. Bows are lighter and stronger, and some are more complex. If your child is interested in bow hunting, or you want your child to learn how to bow hunt, you have come to the right place. You must remember that the equipment helps your child, but it is skill and knowledge of the game that will take your child a long way. These skills may take years to develop, and therefore, it is best to start teaching your child how to bow hunt at an early age.

Over the course of this book, you will gather information on why you should introduce bow hunting to your kids, the required equipment, and some tips and safety measures that you must keep in mind. There are also some laws that you need to teach your children to ensure that they know how to protect an animal. So, let's get started.

Chapter One: Why Should You Learn How To Bow Hunt?

People do not plan to become survivors, and hence they do not want to learn a survival skill. Parents protect their children from harm. It is because of this that most children do not worry about developing a survival skill. They will go back to sleep if the lights go out and not worry about what they should do to ensure that they are safe. If you are reading this book, the chances are that you want to teach your child how to bow hunt.

So, ask your children this – what would they do if a zombie apocalypse really did happen? How will they procure food? Will they learn to hunt then? They may have guns in hand, but the bullets will disappear. If they know how to bow hunt, they can always use different materials to make a bow and some arrows. It is best to train your children to focus on tracking and stealth hunting. These are the most valuable skills that your child can learn.

This chapter covers five reasons why it is important to learn how to bow hunt.

You Will Never Starve

This is the most important reason why children must learn how to hunt with a bow. They will never starve. When they learn how to kill any animal with a bow, they will never be concerned about eating Twinkies or chocolates. They can also learn how to hunt large animals like the whitetail deer, since these animals are easy to clean and cook in the wild. A large group of people can also consume these animals.

If you do not want your child to hunt an animal, you can teach him or her to use the bow and arrow to catch fish. If they do not know how to shoot a fish in the water, you can ask them to use a spear.

You Have Protection

If the world were to change in a heartbeat, your child will not have to depend on the policemen or the firemen to save him. If there was a famine in your area, you know that people will come into your home and steal your food. They may also kill you if you refuse to give them food. If your aim is to survive, you can use the bow and arrow as your first line of defense.

It is a DIY Project

The greatest thing about learning how to hunt with a bow is that you do not have to own a bow. You can make them easily, and if your child learns how to shoot, he can also learn how to make a bow. You only need to use a few materials to make a bow and arrow. To make a bow in any situation, you need some hardwood. You can use small sticks as arrows and you can make the head of the arrow using a stone chip. You can also use glass to make a broad head (which is the head of the arrow). Rocks and other debris also make good broad heads. You can also use computer parts, keys and many other things to make an arrowhead. It is difficult to find a string for the bow, but you can use strong plants, vines, or the threads from clothes.

Strings Are Multi-Purpose

Regardless of whether you use a traditional bowstring or you are improvising with something in the wild, you can use it for many other things. For example, you can use a bowstring in a trap, to make a snare or even start a fire through a bow drill. If you find a good source of materials to make the bowstring, you can create different things. You can use the string from the bowstring to build any other object as long as the string is not damaged.

If you plan to use substances like a string to build gear or other objects, you must know how much you have with you and use the string accordingly.

Long Range Damage

There are many weapons in the world, but the bow and arrow are the best weapons to use if you need to hunt an animal that is far away. You can use a bow and arrow from at least 100 yards away. You can never do this if you use a spear or a gun. This means that you can either scare away a predator or kill your prey without getting too close to it.

Now you know why it is important to learn how to hunt with a bow. You can defend yourself in any situation, hunt prey, or use it for a variety of other reasons. If your child goes away for camp, you know that he or she can protect himself because they know how to build and use a bow.

Chapter Two: Equipment Needed for Bow Hunting

Now, that we know why it is important for children to learn to hunt with a bow, let us look at the equipment that your child must own. You can also speak to the instructor if you are uncertain about the bow your child will need to use.

Long Bow

The Long bow is one of the traditional types of bows that people use. You may have seen these bows in old movies. A traditional long bow is made from only one piece of wood. Modern long bows are made from strips of laminated wood with a leather or string grip. If you want your child to have the traditional archer experience, you can purchase this type of bow for him or her. Since this is the most basic type of bow, it adds some exciting challenges.

Traditional Recurve or Olympic Bows

This is one of the first evolutions of the long bow. This bow is made from wood and has limbs that curve into it. If your child owns a bow with a short limb, the arrow he or she releases using that bow will have more energy. Recurve bows are also made using machined aluminum. The recurve bow also has a shelf where the archer can rest the arrow. This will increase the flight of the arrow. Most archers who compete in a variety of competitions use this type of bow.

Compound Bow

A compound bow is one of the best bows available today. In this bow, a pulley or an eccentric cam is mounted at the end of the limb in the bow. Compound bows allow the archer to reduce the weight of the bow by at least 80% using the let-off point on the bow. When the archer reduces the weight of the bow, he or she can remain in the full draw position for a long period.

Arrows

You can let your child choose the arrows he or she would like to shoot. You should let them know that they should choose the arrow depending on which bow they are using. An archer can choose from the following types of arrow:

1. Cedar arrows

2. Fiberglass arrows

3. Aluminum/carbon arrows

4. Aluminum/carbon composite arrows

If your child is using a long bow, they should choose cedar arrows. Otherwise, they can use other types of arrows.

Archery Accessories

There are some accessories that you can use to improve your child's experience when he is bow hunting. Purchase the following to protect your child:

1. A finger-tab or glove to protect your child's fingertips from being chafed when they draw the string back to let the arrow loose.

2. An arm guard to protect your child's forearms from being struck when they release the bowstring.

3. A quiver to hold the arrows he or she will use.

4. A chest protector to prevent your child's clothing from coming in his or her way. This also protects your child from an injury to the chest.

If your child wants to use the compound bow, you should purchase a mechanical release. If your child uses this device, he will not have to release the arrows. The mechanical release can nock and release the arrows. All your child needs to do is press the trigger when the bow is at full draw. The device will release the arrow.

Clothing

Ensure that your child is wearing clothing that will suit the environment that he or she is in. If your child is shooting in winter, ensure that he or she wears warm clothes. Otherwise, he can wear airy clothes. Regardless of the type of clothes your child wants to wear, you have to ensure that there is no piece of clothing that will be caught in the string or by the arrow. Tie your child's hair back and remove any necklaces or place them under their clothing. You should also remove any piercings that may be caught in the bowstring. Also, remove any bracelets/watches from your child's bow arm. Ensure that your child is wearing appropriate footwear for the terrain and weather. Ensure that your child does not wear open footwear since this leaves their flesh exposed to injury from the arrows on the ground.

Camouflage

Camouflage and bow hunting go hand in hand. Camouflage will help the bow hunter remain unseen or unsuspecting when they are hunting prey. If your child is unsure of what clothes to wear, you can ask the instructor or an expert at the sporting-goods store about what clothes your child can wear. Regardless of what your child chooses to wear, you must ensure that he or she is dressed in layers. Bow hunting is a sweaty and vigorous activity, and there are times when your child may have to wait for a long time in the cold.

Chapter Three: Tips to Become a Better Hunter

If you want your child to become a better bow hunter, you should read the following tips:

Be Patient

This is one of the most valuable pieces of advice that you can give your child. They may get antsy and may not want to hunt if they are unable to find their prey. You must ensure that they stay for longer or until they have hit their prey. They should also learn that just because prey does not show up on one day, it does not mean that prey will not show up the next day. Ensure that your child is not discouraged because they were unable to shoot an animal. They need to have more experience in the woods and also learn to put more time into their hunt.

Know the Land You Hunt

It is important for your child to know the land he or she is hunting in, and look at different trails that the animals will travel in. That way they will know where they should set their bow up. You can make it an adventure and teach your child how to use trail cameras to know whether their prey is still in the area. These cameras will also help your child know whether the prey have changed their path or not.

Pull It Up

Ask your child to identify a way to make it easy for him or her to pull the bow in and out when they are hunting. You can use a string or a rope that has a plastic clasp at the end. You can purchase these from a local retailer. This rope will make it easier for your kid to use his bow. He will no longer need to lug it out of the stand when he needs to use it. Ensure that your child does not use a white rope.

It is always best to use dark shades to ensure that the prey does not identify you. Let us assume that your child is hunting a deer, and he uses a white rope for his bow. When the wind blows, the deer may notice the string and run away from the area. Alternatively, you can ask your child to tie the rope to a tree so he or she does not have to worry about it.

Hunt the Wind

A downwind can mess up a hunt. Your child should be made aware that the wind always makes a difference. Your child should learn to pay attention to the direction of the wind regardless of where he or she is hunting. Many hunters do not do this, and never carry a wind-detection tool. Let your child know that he or she must use a wind detection tool even if there is a slight wind in the area.

Shoot More

Ensure that your child practices shooting. You must let them know that they should make their first shot count when they practice. When the moment comes, and an animal is in your child's line of sight, he or she only has the first shot to maim the animal. Encourage your child to mimic a hunting situation at home or in the field. Ask your child to wear the same clothes that he or she would wear on a hunt, including the safety gear.

Hunt Safe

Make sure that your child wears a safety harness. There is a possibility that your child may fall off a tree if he or she does not wear a harness. You can also ask your child to wear a lifeline when he or she is climbing up or down a tree.

Spray Away

Ensure that your child does not smell too bad when he or she steps out for a run. Human odor can ruin a hunt. You must ensure that your children's feet are sprayed well. There are times when an animal will run away from your child even if the wind is in their favor. This is because they can smell your child's boots. Therefore, you must ensure that your child is fully sprayed down.

Play It Smart

Your child must know when it is the season to hunt different animals. If your child is hunting early during the season, they should never invade the territory. If an animal's territory is invaded, it will not only mess the season up for you but will also chase the animal off your property. You should remember that an animal is not stupid. If the animal knows that it is being hunted, it will run away. This will decrease the opportunity to kill the animal.

Pay Attention

Always ensure that your child is paying attention to the animals they are hunting. Animals will come from every direction. Your child should learn to take advantage of the time he or she has in hand and monitor the woods. Only then will your child catch the trophy deer or buck! Do not let your child carry any toys or electronic devices since they are addictive.

Stay Sharp

You should ensure that your child uses a broad head that has a large diameter. These types of broad heads can cut deep and wide, which means that they will kill more effectively. This way, you can follow the trail left by the animal. Experts recommend the NAP Spitfire broad head. You should remember that every bit will help.

Chapter Four: Safety Measures

Let us look at some of the safety measures that you and your child must keep in mind when they are hunting with a bow.

Safety Education Courses

Ensure that you and your child take up a safety education course. The goal of these courses is to protect the hunter from accidents. These courses also teach a hunter his or her responsibilities and their role in the conservation of animals. There are two parts to these programs – the knowledge session and the skills session. The skills session is usually conducted with an exam. Most sessions cover the information listed below:

1. The ethics that a hunter should follow

2. A hunter's responsibilities

3. How bows work

4. Bow safety

5. Wildlife Identification and survival

6. First-aid skills

7. How to handle the crossbow and bow

8. Hunting techniques

9. Rules and information about hunting that is unique to the area

Safety While Manipulating Weapons

Your child must keep the following points in mind when he or she is manipulating their weapon.

Always Point the Broad Head in a Safe Direction

Your child should learn to control the direction of the broad head at all times. Ensure that the bow is not pointed at a target that your child does not intend to shoot. The broad head should never rest on his or her feet. Ensure that the finger is always removed from the trigger guard until your child is ready to fire the arrow. There is a safety on the bow, which will prevent the sudden release of the arrow. Your child should not use that as a substitute for bow handling.

Treat Every Crossbow with the Same Respect

Your child should always aim the crossbow in the right direction the minute he or she picks it up. He or she should also check if an arrow is nocked and the flight track area is clear. If your child is unsure of how to determine if a crossbow is cocked or not and has the safety on, ask the instructor to help your child. Alternatively, tell your child to never accept a crossbow or a bow from someone until the person has shown them that the safety is on.

Be Sure of the Target

This is an important factor to keep in mind. As a hunter, your child must be aware of his or her target. You should tell your child to never lift the bow and aim at a point until they are sure of the target. You can ask them to use binoculars to determine the target and see what is in front and behind the target. This way they can ensure that they do not harm anything else. Since nobody knows what is on the other side of a mountain or ridge, tell your child to never shoot at an animal. Always test how far and fast the arrow travels. You must also ensure that your child does not shoot at a stationary target or at water. The arrow may ricochet which will lead to injury.

Unstring Conventional Bows When Not In Use

You must store the arms when you are traveling to and from a shooting area or hunting ground. Tell your child to remove the bolts and learn how the machines work. You must also instruct them to store the equipment in a cool and dry place.

Firing Range Safety

If your child is practicing or learning how to hunt with a bow in a club, he or she will need to go through the safety rules for the club. There are some rules that are universal to all firing clubs:

1. Obey all the range signs and commands.

2. Only shoot at authorized targets.

3. Un-nock or un-cock the weapon when you are asked to cease-fire.

4. Never handle weapons when there are other people at the range.

5. Firing can only be done from the assigned firing position or line.

6. Always ensure you are safe on the range.

Law Requirements and Safety

Provinces, states, and countries have laws of their own when it comes to the purchase of any shooting weapon. You must ensure that you have gathered all the information necessary to purchase a bow for your child. For example, people in the USA will need to be aware of what is legal in a state and what is not.

Safety of the Hunter

Your child must respect the basic safety principles when he or she is tracking, stalking or waiting for prey. The first condition is that you need to be healthy to walk in the hunting ground or crawl next to prey. You must ensure that your child is fit.

Regardless of which method your child uses, there are safety procedures that you should be aware of. That being said, there are a few common rules of safety that your child should pay attention to:

1. Ask your child to check his or her equipment before the hunt and ensure that everything is working properly.

2. If your child is using new equipment, ensure that you test the equipment. You can ask your child to tune the equipment to his or her liking.

3. Ensure that the target your child is shooting at is an animal. Ask him or her to use binoculars to do so.

4. Tell your child to never shoot an animal if there is a human being next to the animal.

5. Ask your child to look beyond the target to ensure that he or she can release the arrow without any apprehension or worry.

6. Ask your child to never shoot at a sound or

movement. He or she should be aware of where they are shooting.

7. Ask your child to hunt with a partner. You can accompany your child too. This is to ensure that the hunter is safe.

8. Tell your child to be sure that the animal he or she shot is dead before they put the animal in the vehicle. If your child cannot track the animal, alert the authorities.

9. Tell your child to check the equipment and belongings before he or she leaves the ground. You do not want them to bring any unwanted animals to your house.

Chapter Five: Bow Hunting Animal Conservation

Hunter's Role in Wildlife Conservation

Wildlife is a renewable resource with excess supply and, thus, hunters can help to control it to a certain extent in order to establish a healthy balance and conserve their natural habitat. Hunting that is regulated will not lead to endangerment of wildlife species.

Hunting is a good wildlife management technique and hunters play a key role in it by giving an account of the field to wildlife managers.

The funding acquired from hunting licenses given to game and non-game species has helped many populations from dwindling.

Hunters and Wildlife Conservation

Hunters tend to spend more time and money on wildlife conservation compared to any other group in society. Additionally, they also help to sustain the population apart from partaking in the harvesting of excess animals. Here are some of the activities that hunters take part in:

- Filling questionnaires

- Filling surveys

- Stopping at hunter check stations

- Providing samples from harvested animals

- Funding wildlife management through license fees

It is a fun fact to know that no animal in North America has become extinct owing to sport hunting.

The Wildlife Manager's Role in Hunting

The wildlife manager's role is to make sure a certain number of animals are maintained in a specific habitat or slightly under such that no damage is caused to the animals or the habitat. It can be said that a wildlife manager's role is similar to that of a rancher. Ranchers are given the responsibility of limiting the number of animals in a herd to an extent the habitat can tolerate, and wildlife managers will try to maintain the number of animals in balance with their natural habitat. They will also look at the number of species that are breeding in the habitat and ensure that there is a correct balance between young animals and adults in order to maintain balance.

In order to maintain the habitat, the wildlife manager will look at historical trends and current habitat conditions along with the breeding population and any long-term projections and the success of breeding. Using this information, wildlife managers will engage in a variety of practices in order to maintain the balance in the natural habitat.

Wildlife Management Practices

Monitoring Wildlife Populations

Wildlife managers are constantly monitoring the birth and death rate of different species and the condition of their habitat. This information can provide the data needed to find the number of animals that can exist in the natural habitat so that the species can be conserved.

Habitat Improvement

As and when succession takes place, there will be a change in the habitat and the number of animals that can be supported. Wildlife managers will try to cut down or burn the forested areas to promote new growth and slow down the rate of succession. This practice can help to increase the production of specific wildlife species.

Hunting Regulations

Hunting regulations can help to protect the natural habitats and conserve animal population. Regulations can include maintaining daily time limits and bag limits and undertaking legal practices to conserve wildlife.

Hunting

Hunting is a good way to control wildlife population. Hunting practices can help to control wildlife and keep animal population in control. Hunting can provide a good habitat for wildlife management.

Predator Control

Controlling predators can help wildlife populations to remain stable, especially endangered species. Some types of predator control can include predator trapping and hunting.

Artificial Stocking

Restocking of animals is a successful mission in many parts of the country. Trapping game animals where there are excess and releasing them in areas where they are sparse can make for effective restocking practices.

Controlling or Preventing Diseases

The spread of diseases can negatively impact wildlife. Avian cholera is a disease that can affect ducks and geese and other birds of winters. Wildlife managers have the responsibility of finding their carcasses and burning them to control the spread of the disease.

Terms to Understand

Birth Rate

This refers to the number of young animals that are born to females of a specific species over the course of a year.

Death Rate

This refers to the number of deaths in a specific species over a course of one year.

Pittman–Robertson Act

This was approved in 1937 by congress and provides funding to select, restore, and improve wildlife habitat for wildlife management.

Predators

Animals that kill other animals for food.

Succession

This refers to the natural replacement of vegetation or wildlife by other vegetation or wildlife population in a predictable way such as trees and grass grown for wildlife and using them as ground cover.

Beneficial Habitat Management Practices

- Planting food plots

- Performing controlled burning

- Creating brush piles

- Cutting trees

- Pruning/thinning

- Ditching

- Creating diking/levees

- Controlling weeds and predators

- Controlling brush or grass growth through mechanical means

- Creating watering holes

- Enhancing soil (fertilizing and liming)

- Creating wetlands

- Restoring streams

- Creating nest boxes

Balancing Act

Habitats should maintain a balance to support wildlife. It is necessary to maintain a good balance and not remove some population of plants and animals from their habitat and community as that can lead to damage in the community. This tends to happen when urban development occurs and takes over natural habitat.

Developing Wildlife Identification Skills

It is important to develop wildlife identification skills for all hunters - young and old. If you make a mistake, then it can lead to illegal harvesting of game and non-game animals. It is important to recognize game correctly and you must learn to identify the key characteristics of the animals that you are hunting.

Identifying the animals correctly can prove to be challenging. In some cases, the difference between animals of the same species can be subtle including the size of their ears or their coloring.

Many species are protected from being hunted as they can be less in number and do not produce in excess to be hunted or harvested.

Glossary

1. Arm Guard: The protective arm covering for the bow arm.

2. Bare Shaft: Arrows without fletchings.

3. Barebow: A bow with no aiming or sight devices.

4. Bow-scale: Device used to measure the weight of the bow when drawn.

5. Bow-square: Device used to measure the nocking-point position and bracing height.

6. Brace height: Distance between the pivot-point and string of the bow.

7. Cam: Eccentric puller found in compound bows.

8. Chest-guard: Protective covering to prevent the bowstring from catching on your body or clothes.

9. Crest: the colored markings on the shaft of

the arrow.

10. Draw: Pull the Bowstring

11. Draw length: The distance between the pivot point and string at full draw.

12. Fletching: The colored plastic or feathers attached to the end of the arrow.

13. Grip: The place where the hand is kept on the riser.

14. Nock: A plastic device on the arrow through which the string is placed.

15. Overdraw: The device that allows archers to use shorter arrows.

16. Broadhead: Arrow used in bowhunting.

17. Shaft: Body of an arrow.

18. Sling: The device attached to the bow-hand.

Conclusion

Thank you for purchasing the book.

Bow hunting is a challenging and interesting sport that people have started to take an active interest in. For anybody to become a great hunter, he or she should master the skills required to be a bow hunter. This means that anybody will need to practice bow hunting from a tender age. It is for this reason that you should begin to learn how to hunt with a bow when you are a child.

If you want your child to learn how to bow hunt and are looking for ways to make it easier on them, you have come to the right place. This book will provide you with all the information you need to help your child master the art of bow hunting.

Manufactured by Amazon.ca
Acheson, AB

16530194R00028